THE
HOLLY
AND THE
IVY

When Christmas's tide comes in like a bride,
With holly and ivy clad,
Twelve Days in the year much mirth and good cheer
In every household is had.

THE HOLLY

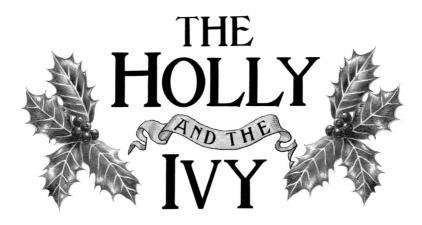

AND THE

IVY

A Celebration of Christmas

BARBARA SEGALL

CLARKSON POTTER/PUBLISHERS
NEW YORK

This book is for my parents, remembering many a
Happy Christmas

Published by Clarkson N. Potter, Inc.,
201 East 50th Street, New York, New York 10022.
Member of the Crown Publishing Group.

Published in Great Britain by Ebury Press in 1991

Clarkson N. Potter, Potter and colophon are trademarks of Clarkson N.
Potter Inc.

Manufactured in Italy

Design Polly Dawes
Editor Jude Welton
Photographer Derek St Romaine
Holly and ivy paintings Benjamin Perkins
Holly and ivy border Sally Hynard
Holly and ivy garland Anne Dyball
Endpapers design copyright by Cranston Print Works Company, V.I.P. Fabrics Division

Library of Congress Cataloging-in-Publication Data Available

ISBN 0-517-58609-6

10 9 8 7 6 5 4 3 2 1

Printed and bound in Italy by New Interlitho S.p.a., Milan

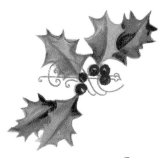

CONTENTS

Introduction

OUR pre-Christian ancestors appreciated the magical qualities of the Holly and the Ivy, two plants which bore fruit in the deep midwinter. By garlanding their homes with berry-laden, shining, green-leaved sprigs of holly and ivy, they drew closer to the power and the hope that these plants represented.

Today, when we bring holly and ivy into our homes at Christmas or send greetings' cards adorned with their images, we keep alive traditions that we instinctively feel to be important, but only half understand. Holly and ivy came in from the cold long, long before the first Christmas of all. They brightened the year's end for Druids, ancient Greeks and Romans and, eventually, for the early Christians. In this book, we follow their journey and discover the magic that surrounds them.

Holly and ivy appear in many guises at Christmas. They are our favourite Christmas decorations, welcoming us in the form of door wreaths, mantelpiece garlands, generous swags and traditional kissing boughs. As design motifs, they have enriched textiles, ceramics and decorative art throughout the world, making a delightful collection theme. The carols and poems we sing at Christmas are filled with their rich symbolism. After the Christmas festivities are over, we can enjoy holly and ivy in gardens, balconies and (for ivy) the most modern of apartment interiors. The leaves of common holly (*Ilex aquifolium*) and ivy (*Hedera helix*) are so distinctive that they are said to be the only leaves that street-wise urban children can recognise. The paintings, by Benjamin Perkins, which open each chapter of our story introduce some of my own favourites from the hundreds of holly and ivy plants that gardeners can treasure all through the year.

At Christmas, I believe, we return unconsciously to the myths of renewal and hope that these two plants stand for. Forty years before the birth of Christ, the Roman poet Virgil felt the stirring of that legendary association:

Unbidden Earth shall wreathing Ivy bring

And fragrant herbs (the promises of Spring)

As her first offerings to her infant King.

Many thanks are due to holly and ivy experts and enthusiasts world-wide; to my family and friends for holly and ivy gifts in years past - and to come, I hope !

B.J.S.

Holly Cottage.

A Merry Christmas

CHRISTMAS MAGIC

Green grow'th the holly,
    So doth the ivy;
Though winter blasts blow ne'er so high,
    Green grow'th the holly.

Green grow'th the holly,
    So doth the ivy;
The God of life can never die,
    Hope! saith the holly.

Attributed to King Henry VIII (1491-1547)
From a 16th century English carol.

F all the trees that are in the wood, the holly and the ivy come into our lives forever linked as symbols of a traditional Christmas. They have gathered myths and legends wherever they grow. At the heart of the matter, theirs is a story about new life. Pagans, first, and then early Christians were awe-struck by these plants that remained green of leaf and ripe of berry when all else is bare in a northern midwinter. They have always been talismans of rebirth, a sign that spring is near.

So it is not surprising that traditions grew up in which both plants were consulted to discover where life and particularly love might lead in the year ahead. Once, not so long ago, for example, a young Scottish lass might walk the lanes before Christmas dreaming of her unknown love. Having picked a single leaf of ivy and laid it next to her heart, she would recite the magic words:

Ivy, ivy, I love you,
In my bosom I put you,
The first young man who speaks to me
My future husband he shall be.

A similar romantic tradition existed in Ireland's County Leitrim but in this case it was the young men who sought to know their prospects. They had to gather ten

Best wishes for Christmas

ivy leaves in total silence, cast one away, then place the nine that remain under a pillow for dreams of love and marriage to follow. Holly and ivy can also advise whether a choice of partner is a wise or lucky one. Float a single holly leaf bearing a tiny candle across a bowl of water. If it capsizes, it is time to forget the fellow. Simpler still, fingertips tapped round a holly's prickles discover 'will he? won't he?'.

Ivy's predictions are a little more dramatic. Take two leaves, one smooth in outline and one indented. The first represents the girl; the second the boy. Cast the leaves on the Christmas fire and see if they jump towards or apart from each other.

The sexual symbolism of our companion plants has a long pedigree. Traditionally, the smooth-leaved, cling-ing ivy symbolises woman, while prickly holly denotes man. This medieval carol focuses on the spirited rivalry between the two:

> Holly and Ivy made a great party,
> Who should have the mastery,
> In landes where they go.

> Then spake Holly, 'I am free and jolly.
> I will have the mastery,
> In landes where we go.'

> Then spake Ivy, 'I am lov'd and prov'd.
> And I will have the mastery,
> In landes where we go.'

> Then spake Holly, and set him down on his knee,
> 'I pray thee, gentle Ivy,
> Say me no villainy,
> In landes where we go.'

Some people believe that this song is a relic of one of the Christmas plays performed by travelling players. Such ritual battles of the sexes, as symbolised by holly

and ivy, were widespread. One surprised traveller in the county of Kent, England, came across a curious ceremony one St Valentine's Day in the 1700s. ' The girls from five or six to eighteen years old were assembled in a crowd, burning an uncouth effigy which they called a "holly boy", and which they had stolen from the boys; while in another part of the village the boys were burning what they called an "ivy girl", which they had stolen from the girls. The ceremony of each burning was accompanied by acclamations, huzzas and other noise.' Unfortunately, no-one in the village could remember what the custom meant.

The ritual battle of the sexes which was fought on St Stephen's Day, December 26, was less jolly. They called it Holming Day (holm being an ancient name for holly). Holming involved the men and boys giving the girls' bare arms a whacking with holly branches. The bizarre custom survived in Wales until the 1800s.

Holly and ivy held their ancient place in ritual, despite centuries of Christian shaping, but the key is lost that would unlock some of these old ceremonies. Who knows why the strongest man in the town of Brough, in Yorkshire, England, carried a flaming holly tree through the town's streets on Twelfth Night? Gangs from rival inns contested for the embers to take back as trophies. Who understands why the 'Green Man', wearing his wooden frame stuck with holly and ivy, danced each year to the May Pole with a retinue of young sweeps? The answers were probably lost when the early Christian Church, knowing a strong symbol when it saw one, began to claim holly. Does not its very name mean holy, the monks suggested? It does not: it derives from the Anglo Saxon name for the

tree, *holegn*. But the obvious association of holly's red berries with Christ's blood was easy to assert. So we find a legend from Brittany, France, explaining that the robin earned its red breast as it tried to pluck holly's prickles from Christ's crown of thorns. Another tale recounts that holly first grew berries when a lamb, following its shepherd to the manger where Jesus lay, was caught on holly's tough and prickly leaves.

Even though the Church neutralised its pagan power, holly never lost the identity that its natural defensive prickliness gives it. In about the year 70 AD the Roman naturalist, Pliny the Elder noted holly's protective power. Throw a holly stick at a mad dog and it will calm down at once, was his considered advice.

Eighteen hundred years later, the Native Americans of Pennsylvania, USA, pinned holly sprays to their clothes when they went to battle: holly was their red badge of courage. And in the gentler world of Devonshire, England, holly

Wishing you
A Happy Christmas.

continued to protect young ladies from supernatural powers even in 1893, when *The Lady* magazine reported: 'Our West Country girls have a pretty custom of trimming their beds with holly on Christmas Eve. They say the evil spirits will harm them if they omit this Christmas ceremony.'

Holly traditionally defends against ill-health, as well as against physical and spiritual dangers. In North Carolina, USA, it was once a custom to heal a sick child by making a split in a holly tree, wedging it open and passing the child through the gap. Then the tree would be filled with clay, and bound. As the tree healed, so would the child. Exactly the same custom is known from Russia and England.

Although a powerful protector, holly became an equally powerful purveyor of bad luck if cut at any time except Christmas. Even today, few people are so foolhardy as to fell a holly tree (which is one reason why many survive as lone sentinels in hedgerows).

Ivy, like holly, has a reputation for bringing mixed fortunes. In 1969, a cook in London resigned rather than work in a home that gave ivy house room! That was a rare survival of prejudice, for ivy is one of the most popular houseplants. Nevertheless, in the state of Maine, USA, there was once a belief those who kept ivy indoors would always be poor.

The medieval Church kept ivy at a distance, in case of ill-luck, as a Christmas carol of the 1400s records:

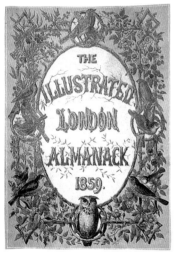

'Holy stond in the hall,
Fayre to behold.
Ivy stond without the dore
She ys full sore a-cold.
Holy and his mery men,
They dawnsyn and they syng.
Ivy and hur maydens,
They wepyn and they wryng'.

Yet ivy has a merry role to play at Christmas too, since it has a legendary association with alcohol. In Roman times, Pliny the Elder reported that ivy berries, taken before drinking, prevented drunkenness, and that steeping ivy leaves in wine had a similar effect. Pliny's prescription is echoed in the old saying 'good wine needs no bush' - the bush in question being an ivy bush (a garland of ivy hung round a wooden frame). Good wine, the theory was, would not give you a hangover, and did not need protection by ivy. It followed that an ivy bush hanging outside an inn was a sign to travellers of good cheer within. Many inns were named after the ivy bush (the Old Bull and Bush was one of them). Ivy's association with wine dates back to

ancient Egyptian myth, and in the classical Greek and Roman world to Dionysus, or Bacchus. As god of wine, ivy and laurel he was worshipped in rites at which intoxicated priestesses, ivy twined in their hair, danced wildly.

In myth, Bacchus died but was resurrected. In Christian faith, Christ's triumph over death is celebrated at the Church's greatest festival, Easter. At Christmas, both our chosen plants express the everlasting promise of renewal and new life.

THOMAS SMITH & COMP.

ILLUSTRATED CATALOGUE

OF

CHRISTMAS NOVELTIES

SEASON
1882-83

DECORATIONS

Deck the halls with boughs of holly,
    'Tis the season to be jolly,
Don we now our gay apparel,
    Troll the ancient Yuletide carol.

See the blazing Yule before us,
    Strike the harp and join the chorus,
Follow me in merry measure,
    While I tell of Yuletide treasure.

Traditional Welsh carol.

A HAPPY,
NEW-YEAR.

*T*HE wreaths and garlands of Christmas are our way of bringing the magic of the greenwood into our homes. When holly and ivy are gathered for Christmas decorations the sprites of the forest come too, with an elf or a fairy peeping out from behind every single leaf.

Tradition holds that during the twelve days of Christmas, there is a truce between humans and the spirit world. But take care on Twelfth Night for then every last leaf must be out of the house as the truce is over.

The early Fathers of the Christian Church rightly suspected that people who hung up Christmas decorations were dancing to an older, pagan tune.

'Make not a temple of thy own house door', warned one priest, watching the early Christians pinning up their garlands just as the ancient Romans had done at the turn of the year to mark their feast for Saturn, god of agriculture, and the New Year festival of the Kalends. In 610 AD, a Church Council banned the adornment of houses with 'green boughs' and many centuries later the

Puritan Fathers of New England were just as stern. There, Christmas greenery and festivity were frowned upon until the 1800s.

Despite such periods of suppression, the traditional seasonal decoration of the house with holly and ivy continued, gathering local customs and lore as time passed. In some places cutting the branches of holly and trails of ivy and bringing them home was man's work. In

England's Oxfordshire in the 1670s it was the convention 'For the maidservant to ask the man for ivy to dress the house, and if the man denies, or neglects to fetch in the ivy, the maid steals away a pair of his breeches, and nails them up to the gate in the yard or highway.' It is easy to guess where such games might lead!

In some places complex rituals were thought necessary to ensure that holly brought its luck into the house. One old lady recalled how, in the 19th century, among villages of Yorkshire, England, 'Some folks used to lay a bunch of holly on the doorstep on Christmas Eve, so as to be ready.' Then it was the task of the 'lucky bird' – the first person to enter the house on Christmas Day morning – to bring the holly indoors. The 'lucky bird' had to be male and some stipulated he had to be a boy with dark hair for

the luck to be really effective. Only after his visit could the family leave the house (hands and face unwashed custom dictated) to collect their own evergreens.

As a decoration on its own, ivy's traditional association with Bacchus, god of wine, gave it a special role. A popular song of the 1630s ran :

At Christmas men do a'wayes ivy get,
And in each corner of the house it set ,
But why do they, then use that Bacchus weed?
Because they mean Bacchus-like to feed.

When holly and ivy combine in decorations, the magic grew stronger and more linked to romance. The kissing bough or bunch – one of the loveliest Christmas decorations mixing holly and ivy, was the centre-piece.

In the annals of folklore for England's Derbyshire there is a detailed description of a kissing bunch: 'It is always an elaborate affair. The size depends upon the couple of hoops – one thrust through the other – which form its skeleton. Each of the ribs is garlanded with holly, ivy, and sprigs of other greens, with bits of coloured ribbons and paper roses, rosy-cheeked apples, specially reserved for this occasion, and oranges. Three small dolls are also prepared, often with much taste, and these represent our Saviour, the mother of Jesus and Joseph.... Mistletoe is not very plentiful in Derbyshire; but, generally, a bit is obtainable, and this is carefully tied to the bottom of the kissing bunch.'

The dancing and merriment under the kissing bough in midwinter links Christmas decorations to the fertility rites that, long before the Christian era, led people from year's end to year's end. Today, the bough makes its appearance as a sprig of mistletoe.

By the end of the 19th century, many traditional decorations had found their way to the United States, and commercial observance of Christmas increased year after year. Americans enthusiastically embraced the 'old-fashioned' Christmas expressed in the writings of their own Washington Irving, as well as in Charles Dickens' *A Christmas Carol* and *Pickwick Papers*.

In New York in 1898 large department stores recorded that they had bought 'by actual measurement'

forty miles of garland greenery. A skilled worker, wiring eight-inch overlapping sprays to a length of twine, could make forty yards in an evening. There were also wreaths – 'fancy pieces – shaped into horseshoes, diamonds and crosses. The tradition and enthusiasm continue. North American holly orcharders work through November and December to cut and pack their prickly harvest ready for the Christmas trade.

There is no doubt that our Christmas decorations are enriched by the customs of many peoples. Among the most charming are the 'Christmas tree yards' intro-duced to the United States by early settlers from Moravia in Eastern Europe. These wonderful and elabo-rate fantasy gardens are created with evergreens and miniature buildings set out around the base of Christmas trees. Village landscapes, farmyards and forests evoke memories of the European past.

For many, the door-wreath of holly, ivy, fruits and gilded nuts is the focus of Christmas decoration. It originated in a popular Victorian style of indoor decoration that often framed a seasonal text of welcome. 'We bordered two pictures with bright-berried holly, after frosting it with Epsom Salts' records a Christmas diarist of the 1870s. 'Over the room door rested a scroll, on which one of us had illuminated, "Glory to God in the highest, and on Earth peace, Goodwill towards Men". This was enclosed within a border of holly leaves, one leaf point laid over the base of another'.

However exquisite, the decorations had to come

down on Twelfth Night. In Devonshire, England, folk once kept a little holly until the following year to light the fire to cook the Christmas pudding. In many places farmers thought it brought good luck if they fed the Christmas greenery to the cattle. But out of the house it had to go – and it was specially important to get those lurking woodland sprites out of the churches. Servants were sent to church to sweep every leaf from the pews:

> For look how many leaves there be
> Neglected there (maids trust to me)
> So many goblins you shall see.

CARDS AND PRESENTS

The holly's up, the house is all bright,
The tree is ready, the candles alight:
Rejoice and be glad, all children tonight!

Let every house be ready tonight –
The children gathered, the candles alight –
That music to hear, to see that sight.

P.Cornelius (1824-74) German carol.

A MERRY XMAS

ELIGHT and anticipation always seem to mingle at Christmas, for adults and children alike, as we look for our gifts under the Christmas tree or in stockings at the foot of the bed. Presents are part of a tradition that comes down the centuries to greet us. They are the direct descendants of the gifts that ancient Romans gave each other to mark their New Year festival, the January Kalends.

The Romans called these gifts *strenae* – the French call their New Year's gifts *étrennes* to this day. Roman gifts included a sprig of holly, ivy or other evergreen, carrying wishes for a bright future after winter.

Today our tradition of gifts continues, but instead of exchanging holly and ivy plants we can choose gifts that celebrate their constant companionship on Christmas cards, wrapping paper, textiles, in wood and in porcelain-ware or ceramic-ware. One of the charms of making a thematic collection – antiques or bygones with a unity of subject – is the opportunity to embrace treasures from a host of different periods, styles and countries, yet still create a collection of character.

A fascinating way to start is with the Christmas cards of yesteryear. Glowing with Victorian sentimentality, they are miniature marvels of art and technical skill. For 150 years holly and ivy have ruled supreme on Christmas cards on both sides of the Atlantic. Yet, there was not a scrap of holly or ivy to be seen on the world's first Christmas card, launched with a print run of 1000 in 1843 by an inventive British art enthusiast, Henry Cole. Five years passed before a second design appeared, and this time its artist, William Maw Egley, included holly as a cornerpiece to the festive scene it depicted.

At first, most people thought this new idea would be a passing craze. But they were wrong. The Victorians enjoyed sending cards. They delighted in their vivid colours: indeed, even before Christmas cards were invented, brightly printed scraps featuring Christmas themes of holly and robins were a great success, attached to visiting cards for seasonal visits.

The Victorians took cards seriously, even reviewing new designs in the press. Families began to treasure their personal collections, keeping them in albums and spending many a fireside evening enjoying them.

Holly and ivy managed to cling to their position in pride of place on Christmas card designs, despite strong competition from a host of spring and summer flowers. The reasons behind the unseasonal appearance of these rival blooms lies in the then fashionable 'language of flowers'. Whether they were tongue-tied, shy, chaperoned or sophisticated, young lovers in Victorian days could 'say it with

flowers', since every plant that grew in the garden or hedgerow had a specific meaning.

A wild geranium spoke of steadfast purity and a pansy meant 'you occupy my thoughts'. Little books that listed and unlocked these secrets were popular – one ran to sixty editions between 1820 and 1890. Apart from their age-old links with luck and rebirth, holly and ivy had their own places in this secret flower language: ivy signified friendship, fidelity and marriage, while holly represented foresight.

In cases where holly and ivy were nudged off the Christmas cards by summer flowers, the cards' verses offered excuses to explain the odd collisions between summer and winter plant life depicted on the front of the flower card. These verses appeared on a floral card produced by the firm of Marcus Ward in the 1880s:

Coldly the North Wind is blowing,
Fast beats the snow on the pane,
Darkly the river is flowing,
Yet Summer will come again.
The West Wind's breath will awaken
The blossom on meadow and plain,
Long is the sleep they have taken,
Yet Summer will come again.

Purists were unconvinced, and disapproved of the trend towards these un-Christmas alternatives to the holly and the ivy. In the December issue of *Art Journal* for 1862, the editor was pleased to note that the pile of new offerings sent for review was 'of exceedingly pure and beautiful nature' and, above all, in keeping with the season – 'holly and ivy predominating'.

On both sides of the Atlantic, holly and ivy remained the seasonal favourites. In the 1870s Louis Prang, father of the American Christmas card copyrighted one of his most sought-after designs: it showed six children with white doves, within a frame of holly leaves and berries.

Sometimes it seemed as if the cards were referring back to the pre-Christian associations of the plants. One set of cards from the popular range by the English manufacturer, De la Rue, depicted favourite evergreen Christmas plants as sprites or nymphs. On 'A sprite of

The Ivy' a maid is 'lightly clad in the lightest of drapery', sitting on a swing made of ivy tendrils, and holding a cluster of ivy berries.

As many Europeans started new lives on the other side of the globe, traditional motifs of holly and ivy, rooted in cold northern winters, disappeared each year into chilly postmen's sacks to emerge where Christmas passed in blazing midsummer sunshine. Inevitably, plants more appropriate to those climates have advanced their claims to the honour of representing Christmas. In modern Australia acacia and bottle brush may have replaced holly and ivy for some.

Greetings cards are not the only objects adorned with holly and ivy. Ivy's sinuous lines appealed to ceramic artists since ancient Greek and Roman times. And it has remained a popular motif throughout the centuries. In 1815, ivy made its way on to a porcelain dinner service known as Napoleon Ivy. A green and brown leaf

Christmas Greetings

To Wish you a Happy Christmas

CHRISTMAS·MORNING

WHY, SANTA CLAUS IS KIND, INDEED!
WE NEVER WROTE A LETTER,
AND YET HE'S BROUGHT US ALL WE NEED,
OH, NOTHING COULD BE BETTER !

pattern wreathes richly round each dish and plate. The original service was ordered by the British government for the ex-emperor of France, Napoleon Bonaparte, who was in exile on the island of St Helena. It would have reminded him of his own Sèvres porcelain service with its rich gold ivy wreaths around each rim.

In England, in the mid 1800s, special Christmas tableware brought holly and ivy to the feast. Cheese dishes, cream jugs, mince pie trays, candle sticks and turkey platters were wreathed with holly and ivy patterns. Commemorative plates from the British Midland pottery firms continue this tradition today. The Stoke-on-

Trent firm, Wedgwood, launched a series of commemorative Christmas plates in 1969: pale blue jasper ware
plates, have a central relief of a famous British scene or
building, with a formal border of white holly leaves.

In the 19th century many potteries across Europe
turned to the theme of holly and ivy. One from France –
a Limoges china tea set, delicately patterned with pink
ribbon and holly – was made in the 1890s for the London
department store, William Whiteley's. Also from France
was a robust dinner service with stencilled holly leaves
encircling the edges, once well-used in Normandy farm-
house kitchens.

On a less grand scale, creating a holly-and-ivy collection of china, textiles, jewellery and Christmas
ephemera is within most people's means, and it can form
a treasure-trove table display at Christmas. Unusual
Christmas collectables in the picture opposite include an
ivy-encrusted Victorian brush and a Victorian robin and
holly scene – with the festive message concealed
beneath the robin's silken wing.

Collecting can provide year-round pleasure, and
since most people are blind to holly and ivy outside the
Christmas season, there is a good chance of finding a
bargain to enjoy or to give.

CAROLS AND POEMS

The darling of the world is come,
And fit it is we find a room
To welcome him. The nobler part
Of all the house here is the heart.

Which we will give him, and bequeath
This holly and this ivy wreath,
To do him honour who's our King,
And Lord of all this revelling.

Robert Herrick (1591-1674).

FROM Advent, and through the twelve days of Christmas to Epiphany, carols and poetry tell of the seasonal triumphs of holly and ivy.

THE PRAISE OF CHRISTMAS

When Christmas's tide comes in like a bride,
With holly and ivy clad,
Twelve Days in the year much mirth and good cheer
In every household is had.
The country guise is then to devise
Some gambols of Christmas play,
Whereat the young men do best that they can
To drive the cold winter away.

T.Durfey (1653-1723).

A CHRISTMAS CAROL

CHRISTMAS COMES BUT ONCE A YEAR

Christmas comes but once a year
Those Christmas bells as sweetly chime,
　As on the day when first they rung
So merrily in the olden time,
　And far and wide their music flung:
Shaking the tall grey ivied tower,
With all their deep melodious power:
　They still proclaim to every ear,
　Old Christmas comes but once a year.

Then he came singing through the woods,
　And plucked the holly bright and green:
Pulled here and there the ivy's buds:
　Was sometimes hidden, sometimes seen –
Half-buried 'neath the mistletoe,
His long beard hung with flakes of snow:
　And still he ever carolled clear,
　Old Christmas comes but once a year.

Thomas Miller, 19th century.

AUNT MARY – A CHRISTMAS CHANT

Now of all the trees by the king's highway,
    Which do you love the best?
O! the one that is green upon Christmas Day,
    The bush with the bleeding breast.
Now the holly with her drops of blood for me:
For that is our dear Aunt Mary's tree.

Its leaves are sweet with our Saviour's Name,
    'Tis a plant that loves the poor:
Summer and winter it shines the same
    Beside the cottage door.
O! the holly with her drops of blood for me:
For that is our kind Aunt Mary's tree.

'Tis a bush that the birds will never leave:
    They sing in it all day long;
But sweetest of all upon Christmas Eve
    Is to hear the robin's song.
'Tis the merriest sound upon earth and sea:
For it comes from our own Aunt Mary's tree.

From Robert Stephen Hawker, 1838
In Cornwall Uncle and Aunt were titles of respect:
Aunt Mary is the old Cornish way of addressing Christ's Mother.

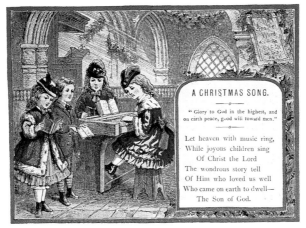

A CHRISTMAS SONG.

"Glory to God in the highest, and on earth peace, good will toward men."

Let heaven with music ring,
While joyous children sing
    Of Christ the Lord
The wondrous story tell
Of Him who loved us well
Who came on earth to dwell—
    The Son of God.

I V Y

Ivy is soft and meek of speech,
    Against all bale she is bliss,
Well is he that may her reach,

Ivy is green, with colours bright,
    Of all trees best she is,
And that I prove will now be right

Ivy beareth berries black,
    God grant us all his bliss,
For there shall be nothing lack.

Traditional carol, early Middle Ages.

ON CHRISTMAS EVE

Carols celebrating the seasonal gathering of evergreens to deck the house, and the return to the fire and holiday merriment are still popular today.

MERRY CHRISTMAS

On Christmas Eve the bells were rung,
On Christmas Eve the mass was sung;
    The damsel donned her kirtle sheen,
The hall was dressed with holly green;
    Forth to the wood did merry-men go,
To gather in the mistletoe:

Then drink to the holly berry,
    With hey down, hey down derry!
The mistletoe we'll pledge also,
    And at Christmas all be merry,
At Christmas all be merry.

The fire, with well-dried logs supplied,
Went roaring up the chimney wide;
    Then came the merry masquers in,
And carols roared with blithesome din.
    England is merry England, when
Old Christmas brings his sports again.

Sir Walter Scott (1771-1832).

HARK! the carol
heavenward floats;
Listen to the liquid notes;
Listen well, and you may
hear
Song of Cherubs hover-
ing near.

ON CHRISTMAS DAY

In this Christmas Day carol, the legends of holly and ivy
are interwoven with the Christian story of the Nativity
and Crucifixion.

HOLY DAY HOLLY CAROL

Now the holly bears a berry as white as the milk,
   And Mary bore Jesus, who was wrapped up in silk:

And Mary bore Jesus Christ our Saviour for to be,
   And the first tree in the greenwood, it was the holly,
   holly, holly!
And the first tree in the greenwood, it was the holly.

Now the holly bears a berry as green as the grass,
   And Mary bore Jesus, who died on the cross:

Now the holly bears a berry as black as the coal,
   And Mary bore Jesus, who died for us all:

Now the holly bears a berry, as blood is it red,
   Then trust we our Saviour, who rose from the dead:

Traditional carol, Cornwall, England.

THE HOLLY AND THE IVY

The holly and the ivy,
When they are both full grown,
Of all the trees that are in the wood,
The holly bears the crown:

The rising of the sun
And the running of the deer,
The playing of the merry organ,
Sweet singing in the choir.

The holly bears a blossom,
As white as the lily flower,
And Mary bore sweet Jesus Christ,
To be our sweet Saviour:

The holly bears a berry,
As red as any blood,
And Mary bore sweet Jesus Christ
To do poor sinners good:

The holly bears a prickle,
As sharp as any thorn,
And Mary bore sweet Jesus Christ
On Christmas day in the morn:

The holly bears a bark,
As bitter as any gall,
And Mary bore sweet Jesus Christ
For to redeem us all:

The holly and the ivy,
When they are both full grown,
Of all the trees that are in the wood,
The holly bears the crown:

The rising of the sun
And the running of the deer,
The playing of the merry organ,
Sweet singing in the choir.

Traditional English carol.

UNDER THE KISSING BOUGH

Christmas is a time for loving. There are Kissing boughs
and many holly-and-ivy ways to tell your future love. And
in poems and carols, the evergreen pair are celebrated
as symbols of constancy.

LIKE THE IVY
True love is like the ivy bold,
That clings each day with firmer hold:
That groweth on through good and ill,
And 'mid the tempest clingeth still.

George Weatherly, 19th century.

TO MY LADY TRUE
As the holly groweth green
And never changeth hue,
So am I, ever hath been,
To my lady true.

As the holly groweth green
With ivy all alone,
When flower cannot be seen,
And greenwood leaves be gone:

Now unto my lady
Promise to her I make,
From all others only
To her I me betake.

Attributed to King Henry VIII (1491-1547).

CANDLEMAS EVE

And when the Christmas party is over, it's time to take down the decorations. At Candlemas, February 2, when the Church celebrates the Presentation of Christ to the Temple, this carol harks back to the holly and the ivy which marked His birth.

CANDLEMAS EVE CAROL

Down with the rosemary and bays,
Down with the mistletoe:
Instead of holly, now upraise
The greener box, for show.

The holly hitherto did sway:
Let box domineer
Until the dancing Easter Day,
Or Easter's eve appear.

Then youthful box, which now hath grace
Your houses to renew,
Grown old, surrender must his place
Until the crisped yew.

When yew is out, then birch comes in,
And many flowers beside,
Both of a fresh and fragrant kin,
To honour Whitsuntide.

Green rushes then, and sweetest bents,
With cooler oaken boughs,
Come in for comely ornaments,
To readorn the house.

Thus times do shift: each thing his turn does hold;
New things succeed, as former things grow old.

Robert Herrick (1591-1674).

THE GARDEN

A garden nook where, all aglow,
The holly glitters, berry-sprent,
And deftly pleached the branches grow,
With shining ivy interblent.

Within the bower a grateful gloom –
The greenly tempered gloom of leaves –
Shot with gleams from that fierce loom
Which all the sunset splendour weaves.

William Sawyer, 19th century.

NOT only at Christmas, but all year round, the holly and the ivy have long been rewarding house and garden guests. And indoors, as the Victorians discovered, ivy has a rare talent to soften the contours and brighten the corners of a room. Garden enthusiasts for the two plants are fascinated by the variety they display. Although English holly (*Ilex aquifolium*) and common ivy (*Hedera helix*) have leaves that are instantly recognisable, the numerous cultivated varieties of these two plant species can differ astonishingly.

For ivy lovers, there are some 400 different ivies to discover for home and garden. More than 100 of them cling to an immense brick wall, 870ft long at Erddig Hall, Clwyd, north Wales: they form one of Britain's two national ivy collections. The other is at the

Northumberland College of Agriculture, Newcastle-upon-Tyne. In the United States at Longwood Gardens, Kennett Square, Pennsylvania, there is a remarkable display of ivies specially trimmed to whimsical topiary shapes – including even life-size carousel animals.

We are still discovering the full extent of the vast holly family. There are over 400 species, and several hundred cultivars known to botanists and gardeners world-wide. They vary in leaf prickle (surprisingly, most species do not have prickly leaves), leaf shape and colour, habit and berry colour. Some 300 specimens of hollies in cultivation grow in Britain's National Holly Collection at the Savill Garden and Valley Gardens of Windsor Great Park, Berkshire. At least 20 American arboreta, among them the United States National Arboretum, Washington D.C., and the Scott Arboretum at Swarthmore College, Pennsylvania, boast fine displays of well-established hollies.

Botanists, specialist growers and gardeners have all contributed to creating new hollies to delight us, but the search continues for a legendary white-berried English holly, much described in the early 1800s, but never reliably recorded since.

The charm of such diversity – holly berries which range from deep red to glowing orange-amber to clear yellow; ivy leaves that can be heart-shaped or frilly-edged, dark or spring green or even marked with milky white or yellow splashes – has inspired their admirers to form national societies. The Holly Society of America, the British Ivy Society and the American Ivy Society welcome new friends, world-wide.

It is a combination of Nature's inventiveness and human's desire to improve on Nature that fills the catalogues of plant nurseries. Just a few decades after the first Christmas, Pliny the Elder noted the ivy's individual

New Year Greetings.

The Grace of God,
so old yet new,
Sustain thee every hour,
And make thee gracious,
kind and true,
By its constraining power!

J. F. H.

differences – observing a grass-green variety 'which is the commonest, a second kind with a white leaf and a third with a variegated leaf'. He also remarked on the ivy berry: 'one kind with black seed and another a seed the colour of saffron, the latter is used by poets for their wreaths'. Almost 20 centuries later, Poet's Ivy *(Hedera helix* var. *poetica)* is still sought after.

Britain has only one dedicated ivy nursery, Whitehouse Ivies, based in the remote Essex village of Tolleshunt Knights. Its proprietor, Ron Whitehouse, dispatches ivies chosen from over 400 species and cultivars to gardens around the world, particularly to Japan, where ivy serves to grace new buildings. For reasons he can only muse upon, one in five of his customers are doctors. In Germany, Brother Ingobert Heieck of Neuberg Abbey tends and offers for sale a similar list.

Long before these two ivy enthusiasts devoted themselves to it, the Victorians had set the plant on the path to decorative glory. Their ivies filled their homes: trailed across screens to make room dividers or were trained along picture rails to provide a living frieze. One of the prized books in gardening history, written by Shirley Hibberd in 1872, and entitled *The Ivy*, sets out the facts and attractions of this versatile plant. Hibberd quotes a Victorian British art student, Mary Howitt, who noted how ivy was used in German homes: 'It is not alone in windows that you see ivy trained. Ivy often forms a green and fresh screen across a room, being planted in boxes, and its sprays trained over rustic framework. Ivy often casts its pleasant shadows over a piano, so that the musician may sit before his instrument as within a little bower.'

The ivy is deservedly the symbol of fidelity and undying love, despite its fickle fancies in form. As ivy grows upwards and matures, it undergoes a transformation, only flowering and bearing berries when it reaches its adult stage and becomes a 'tree ivy'. It is then that its leaves lose their defined, five-fingered ivy-shape and become more rounded. The tiny green flowers, full of nectar, are irresistible to the flies, drowsy wasps and bees of autumn.

The common five-fingered ivy, *Hedera helix* made

its way from Europe to North America where it became known as 'English Ivy'. From this stock, a much branched form sprang. It differed from the usual long vining and trailing habit of ivy. Named 'Pittsburgh', it was launched for the pot plant trade and is undoubtedly the parent of millions of ornamental ivies sold worldwide today.

In the world of holly, there is as rich a range of choice, and once again it is in the United States that many new varieties have been developed.

Give me holly, bold and jolly,

Honest, prickly shining holly

wrote the English poet Christina Rossetti in the 1800s. But, though Americans agreed with her admiration of the holly of Old England, with its glossy green leaf and its brilliant red berry, plantings of English holly did not survive the heavy snows of the East Coast.

With Ivy and laurel,
And bright holly berry,
Be Christmas to you
Both happy and merry!

Even George Washington had trouble establishing holly at Mount Vernon (his diaries have some 20 references to the saga of failure and eventual success). So American enthusiasts created their own

hollies for the gardens of America. In the 1950s, Mrs Kathleen Meserve of New York's Long Island became a notable figure in the holly world. Her hollies, bred on a kitchen windowsill, have become known world-wide as Blue Hollies (*Ilex* **X** *meserveae*), the 'blue' denoting the special glow of their stems. 'Blue Boy', 'Blue Maid' and 'Blue Stallion' are included.

Hollies have a tendency similar to ivy's: a holly's leaf can change shape, losing its distinctive prickles, after the tree has reached a certain height. The 19th-century English poet Robert Southey noted:

Below, a circling fence its leaves are seen
Wrinkled and keen:
No grazing cattle through their prickly round
Can reach to wound:
But as they grow where nothing is to fear,
Smooth and unarmed the pointless leaves appear.'

It is not the only ground for confusion where hollies are concerned. Sex is the other main problem. In relation to its Christmas companion, holly is seen as the masculine partner to feminine ivy. But it is more complicated than

that in the garden.For a start, holly plants can be male
or female and only a few are self fertile. So if your glis-
tening and prickly holly bears no Christmas berries, the
chances are it needs a mate. But beware of being misled
by names: 'Golden King', for example, is a female holly,
while 'Silver Queen' is a male.

Even when the best of partners are nearby, fruition
takes time – a garden holly will not be in berry until it is
at least six years old. And frost can rob you of winter
harvest. Remember – that also means a loss for the birds
in the holly orchard, and along the ivy-clad hedgerows.

WISHING YOU
A MERRY CHRISTMAS

THE HOLLY AND IVY WORLD

Each house is swept the day before,
And windows stuck with evergreens,
The snow besom'd from the door,
And comfort crowns the cottage scenes.

Gilt holly, with its thorny pricks
And yew and box, with berries small,
These deck the unused candlesticks,
And pictures hanging by the wall...

John Clare (1793-1864).

ℐT is a happy chance that Christmas, a worldwide festival, should have two plants that flourish across the globe as its emblems. Ivy lends enchantment to romantic castles in Scotland and softens the contours of the latest palaces of commerce in Tokyo. As for holly, it is found on all continents except one, Antarctica. Even there, fossil holly leaves have been discovered. Hollies grow as brightly in the Himalayas as in Australia.

Thirty million people in South America enjoy holly tea every day. Known as *maté*, it is infused from crushed

leaves of the South American holly. Yet the species most associated with Christmas, English holly, did not occur naturally in one of the parts of the planet where it now thrives so well: the western seaboard of North America.

On the East Coast, there were several native American hollies, *Ilex opaca* among them, to greet the Pilgrim Fathers when they landed. Some of the ancient trees surviving on Cape Cod may be descend-ed from those very trees. But in the West, where mild winters and cool summer nights are English holly's ideal weather, a story waits to be told.

In 1875, an English sea captain brought a pair of English holly trees as a gift to the owner of a salmon cannery in Oregon. From such beginnings, the world's most decorative holly took root so well in Oregon that most folk now think of it as a native tree.

Today you can find English holly orchards that carry on the traditions of pioneering holly farmers from northern California to Vancouver. Orchards specialising in American holly were established at about the same time and are found from Massachusetts to Florida.

A Glorious Christmas

The entire industry was founded on a tree's potent symbolism rather than its fruit or practical use. But holly and ivy do have their uses. The wood of holly – fine, light-coloured and hard-grained (it was often dyed to pass for ebony) – has been turned, in craftspeople's hands, into musical instruments, tomahawks and chariot shafts

As for ivy, it once had a reputation as a herbal remedy. Drinking milk or water from cups made of ivy wood was supposed to cure childhood diseases such as whooping cough and cramp. A potion of ivy twigs boiled in butter was reputed to relieve sunburn.

English holly carries off the prize for decorative virtues: no berry is brighter, no leaf more waxy-green nor more pleasingly prickly. But holly lovers have been sending native American varieties back to Europe for centuries too. A doughty Quaker, John Bartram, was a hero in this business, dispatching to friends in England six varieties never seen in the Old World. He fell out of a tree doing so, and left one of the world's most charming notes of a gardener's mishap. 'I sent him a fine parcel of holly berries ye getting of which I had like to broke my

Fröhliche Weihnachten

bones. I fell on ye top of ye tree where ye top that I had hold of and ye branch that I stood on broke and I fell to ye ground.'

John Bartram was lucky that the tree was not taller, for some holly grows to over eighty feet. The Holly Society of America has a Big Tree Committee that watches over and records the vital statistics of forty famous American holly trees. Among the best loved is the 'B and O' holly (an *Ilex opaca*) that stands by the tracks of the Baltimore and Ohio railway at Jackson, Maryland. From 1948 it became the custom to light this tree each Christmas. Every railway employee wore a sprig of its leaves and berries. Special excursion trains ran trips to the tree, and carols were sung beneath it 'during the twilight and night-time hours', recalled one long-time employee, Pete Hartley.

It was a simple ceremony, far from the ancient world where all this tale began. But wherever and whenever the holly berry brightens Christmas and ivy leaves cling to walls, these two magical companions will keep our Christmas and New Year hopes alive.

ACKNOWLEDGEMENTS

The Bridgeman Art Library:
Cover and main title: Christmas Greetings, Victorian card; **11** Boy in Red in the Snow; **12** The Ivy Garlands; **14** Girl and Boy Carrying Holly: Ethel Parkinson; **15** Holly: Walter Crane/Anthony Crane Collection; **16** (lower right) Wishing You a Happy Christmas: Hanson Collection; **18** The Circle of Love: Eliza Manning (1879-1889); **19** Carrying Home the Christmas Holly; **21** Christmas Time: George Baxter/Maidstone Museum & Art Gallery,Kent; **25** The Christmas Pudding; **26** Decorating the Church: Dickens House Museum, London; **29** Bringing Home the Holly: Edward Smythe (1810-99): Oscar & Peter Johnson Ltd., London; **32** Baby waits for Santa; **33** Christmas Elves; **37** American Christmas card: Victoria and Albert Museum, London; **38** A Merry Christmas: Society of Nativitists, Cardiff; **44** Father Christmas with Toys; **34** Christmas Morning; **50** A Christmas Carol: Victoria and Albert Museum, London; **53** A Christmas Song: Royal Albert Memorial Museum, Exeter; **59** The Huguenot: Sir John Everett Millais (1826-96): Christie's, London; **70** Welcome, Merry Christmas; Royal Albert Memorial Museum, Exeter; **71** Sunday Morning: Florence Hardy; **74** Young Holly Gatherers; **75** Child with Robins; **76** A Glorious Christmas; **77** Father Christmas on the Line: Society of Nativitists, Cardiff; **78** Children Toboganning.

Christmas Archives, Cardiff:
16 (top left) Wishing You a Happy Christmas; **17** Edwardian Card; **20** Cover of *The Illustrated London Almanack*, 1859; **22** Cover of Thomas Smith & Co Catalogue 1882; **24** A Happy New Year; **27** Cover of Thomas Smith & Co list of crackers,1926; **36** A Merry Xmas; **57** Bells and Holly; **39** Girls on Sleds; **64** Winter Gardeners; **68** New year Card, 1880s; **69** With Ivy and Laurel.

The Maurice Rickards Collection:
8 A Merry Christmas; **28** Packaging for Price's Patent Candles; **34** Hearty Wishes; **40** (photograph) (bottom) Goodall card, 1876; **41** (column 1, top card) Angel, Raphael Tuck and Sons; (column 2) The Holly Cart; Rimmel's Almanac Cover 1877; Raphael Tuck & Sons card; Marcus Ward 'Ivy' card; **42** (clockwise, from left, card 2) Christmas stocking; **43** (middle, far right) At the Poulterer's; (bottom row) Christmas Holly Leaf; (bottom row) C & E Layton New Year Robin; **48** Come with Adoration; **55** Carol Singers, Louis Prang & Co; **62** Victorian Christmas scrap; **72** Wishing you a Merry Christmas.

All other illustrations from the collection of **Impress**, London.

The Paintings by Benjamin Perkins: plants identified clockwise from top left. Pages **8-9**: *Hedera helix, Ilex aquifolium* 'Handsworth New Silver' and *Ilex aquifolium*. Pages **22-23**:(1)*I. aquifolium* 'Bacciflava' (2)*H. helix* (Arborescent form) (3)*I. aquifolium* 'Golden Milkboy' (4)*H. helix* 'Glacier' (5)*I. aquifolium* 'Amber' (6)*H. helix* (Arborescent form) (7)*I. aquifolium* 'Golden Queen' (8)*H. helix* 'Goldheart'. Pages **34-35**:(1)*Ilex* X *altaclerensis* 'Belgica Aurea' (2)*H. helix* 'Direktor Badke' (3)'Parsley Crested' (4)'Midas Touch' (5)*I. aquifolium* 'Firecracker' (6)*Hedera hibernica* (7)*Ilex latifolia* (8)*H. helix* 'Fringette'. Pages **48-49**:(1)*H. helix* 'Deltoidea'(2)*I. aquifolium* 'Pyramidalis Fructu Luteo' (3)*H. helix* 'Cathedral Wall' (4)*I* X *altaclerensis* 'Hendersonii' (5)*H. helix* 'Old English' (6)*I.* X *altaclerensis* 'Wilsonii' (7)*H. helix* 'Professor Friedrich Tobler' (8)*I. aquifolium* 'Pyramidalis'. Pages **62-63**:(1)*I. aquifolium* 'Ferox Aurea' (2)*H. helix* 'Ivalace' (3)*I. aquifolium* 'J.C. van Tol' (4)*H. helix* var. *poetica* (5)*I.* X *meserveae* 'Blue Angel' (6)*H. helix* 'Romanze' (7)*I.* X *meserveae* 'Blue Prince' (8)*H. helix* 'Pittsburgh' ((9)*H. helix* 'Atropurpurea' (10)*I. aquifolium* 'Angustifolia. Pages **72-73**:(1)*H. canariensis* 'Margino Maculata' (2)*I. aquifolium* 'Recurva' (3)*H. azorica* (4)*I.* X *altaclerensis* 'Balearica' (5)*H. pastuchovii* (6)*H. colchica* 'Dentata Variegata' (7)(centre left)*I. aquifolium* 'Lichtenthalii' (8) *H. nepalensis* (9) *Ilex opaca*.

We thank Peter Boardman of How Hill Farm, Norfolk, U.K., for holly sprigs and Ron Whitehouse, Whitehouse Ivies, Tolleshunt Knights, Essex, U.K., for young ivy plants. Holly taxonomy and text reviewed by Susyn Andrews, Horticultural Taxonomist at The Royal Botanic Gardens, Kew, who has a long-term interest in the genus *Ilex*. Ivy taxonomy and text reviewed by Peter Q. Rose and Stephen Taffler. Peter Q. Rose is the author of *Ivies* (Blandford), the definitive monograph on the genus *Hedera*. Stephen Taffler is President of the British Ivy Society. We also thank him for the loan of fine examples from his collection of china. We thank Maurice Rickards, Vice President of The Ephemera Society, for reviewing Chapter Three.